Night Shift *in* Perfect English

Mina Khan

GASHER
///////

Gasher Press
www.gasherpress.com

ISBN 978-1-957746-22-7

Cover Art: "Veiller sur" by Andrea "Rea" Kolarova
Cover design by Whitney Koo
Interior design by Whitney Koo

Table of Contents

We look at the world once, in childhood.
The rest is memory.

Louise Glück

and I lived there

on the ride over, someone tells me about crime rates.
not much has changed.

the bedroom plants have yellowed,
and the mattress is missing its sheets.

there's a van that offers a cheap car wash,
and in the summer, a hydrant showers
passing cars

behind my childhood home, there are peppers
that contort
around
the mouth
of a wire fence   me and my mother

took pleasure in studying
what a pepper will do   to remain   as itself.

I am always
more like her.
standing in my own kitchen
on the same plastic stool.

shaking my hips
and humming so loudly. starting stories

in the middle

Night Shift in Perfect English

SCENE

a windowless apartment. somehow, a pathos survives, cluttering around a white-walled living room.

centered is a gorgeous red Pakistani rug, pinned down by two loveseats, still in their plastic cover after twenty years of marriage. the overhead light is cool white.

downstairs and down the street, although the street doesn't matter to this story, is the store.

similarly cluttered, an Upper West Side convenience store in 2008. there is a narrow deli, a machine that slices meat, a loud radio, and an aisle of packaged snacks. metal doors clap in the backdrop.

time is spent between these two spaces.

everything returns to itself

the humid breath of summer.
a mosquito taking its last sip.
and my legs, dotted with notes of it
having ever been alive,
which it was, and will be again, in time.
every life is finite
as it is good, and I
am massive,   heaving
under the weight of someone even larger.
            a mixed pleasure it is
for the mosquito to be splattered.
pushed deeper into the puncture from which it feeds.
for my blood to return to my pores,
itching now, and filtered through another's body.
I have grasped at everything that could be wanted for.
and again, I turn to myself at nineteen.
            do I know the stakes of this?
hot, frail, in endless futile power,
I know, I know, this is the wrong
earth I have been living on,
or, living for: more
more money, more men, more
distance. a branch shakes
by the gust. still feathered in its navy leaves.
everything is true if you say it,
really feel it.   autumn is rolling in
the early patter of rain
round bodies glad   to meet at the pavement.
                              to give way
                        to the heft
      of the evergreen sky

these are just a few

after Melvin Dixon's "And These Are Just a Few...."

Saba is gone. remember Saba? who went by Najir and owned the deli on 106? everyone knew him. he had six pet stores, then five, four and the last one will be closing too. just one store left, stacks of cat food keeling from oversupply...

and remember Kenny? he used to go by Anwar. he ordered one hundred durags because someone asked for one once, and never came back. no one wears durags in this neighborhood, but they did on 103, where everyone knew him, where he had a candy store, a bodega, another in Tribeca...

and remember Bossman? he used to go by Israr. he had a gas station by Javitz where the taxi drivers would break fast. piles of basmati in styrofoam, there were so many prayer mats. green, red, I don't know where he stored them all...

and remember Kim? she used to go by Kwang Soon. owned the deli downtown. flirted with bus drivers over corned beef sandwiches. had a soft spot for apologetic children with screaming parents. always, a scoop of ice cream, a Snickers on the house...

and remember her sister-in-law, Suzie? she used to go by Yoo-Mee. she had a math degree from Gunsan, but worked six days at a restaurant in Queens. she made a lot of friends there, I was the flower girl at a stranger's wedding...

and remember the children? we still remember who they were. before the courthouses, their legal name changes. we remember where they learned to walk, learned to count coins. in the stores, the ones before Amazon, Whole Foods... Seema, Seunghyun, Imran, Irfan, Rehan, Jina....

DRUM

I am every mirror

car ride with papa and he gets a call from a woman, saying his son from another marriage has broken / all the crayons and kicked out her last hard rib / papa says oh no, and hangs / up / town are thick buildings and a long / wet sky I've always looked / up at this woman, who is alive / with thick black hair which I / never learned to braid / because I never learned to be good / at anything / I loved a woman and / she and I broke many things like / our trust and my / mother / Want / wants Loss / my loss grieves / itself / I have gone deft to hone my / apathy / but a child is still in that house with her mom on the floor and a dad heaping over / youth, I loved cherries / my mother was loud / and I cracked / them over the walls and / we all / laughed / I and I and I / all / giddy to be / alive / I don't remember / being young / or being fond / of her just / stories / of stories I've told like: lying in bed, being an age, watching my eyes / adjust to the din / a mother and father / in a thick storied building / swearing / over, I will / remember / this / what it is to be a child / on my own / small earth

I'm bad at cutting mangos

it's tough   around the seed
always too much flesh or
a knife, right into the—/

when her son collapsed, Umma took the double-decker train to
Long Island everyday work,
visitation, and always again

post-op, fresh staples to his scalp. I haven't heard a sound like that

more and more painkillers, and a tolerance still so high

/

when he collapsed, he was cutting me a mango. I asked him
to do it, because I wanted him

off the couch.

when the thud, I wanted

not to notice   greased black hair, his head

streaming the kitchen tiles.

/

anti-seizing medication from a clear orange cylinder.
when papa finally visited,
he stood by the door.

I have seen him cry twice: over the death
of a fish, and his mother. /

/ ice melting in a short plastic cup,

I am witness to such tenderness.

morning

and suddenly, a burst of yellow.
        a yolk against the frame. a child's pleasure
at peeling an egg—
        shell beneath the fingernail,
the paper that attaches,
        and under, a bouncy material,
so far from what I know
        of my own flesh. every
rock dove sounds the same. long
        from its cousin's mourning sighs. I know
too much of this world

SCENE

in her earliest passport photo, she is seventeen. my mother.

when she left Korea, she did so alone. that was when the country was very poor, and everyone hungered.

my mother was the second wave of migrants in the 1980s, of low-educated manual workers to the U.S. my mother worked at factories and fast food restaurants before meeting my father and opening a bodega.

this was an impossible success.

but there is always an after to the American Dream.

I can only know my mother so well. I can listen to stories, and try to map how they interact. I can remember that apartment, the one we shared, albeit through very different bodies. the landscapes she was marred by, the potential in the trees—
otherwise I
      pretend:

a palm reader tells me I will live a long and healthy life

Halmuni has never been to the dentist but
at 87 she still cracks crabs in one bite,
halves legs with her front teeth and
plops pink flesh onto my plate   at the dinner table,

I never speak Korean, flakes of shell
red crunch and strewn about the tablecloth,
her children are American now and
at the nursing home,

no one speaks Korean   Halmuni says it's
drained her blood   all dry inside, she only eats American
now   is the spryest she's ever looked   the other day
nurse didn't help her to the bathroom because

nurse doesn't know the word for 화장실   of course,
Halmuni cracked two ribs, healed in a day,
skin sprung taut, her cheeks undropped
and everyday, she asks when she will finally

before, no one lived to 60.

a reader with good reviews on Google describes my lifeline as
very long and a messy palm and that right now

my energy reads grey-blue anxious and depressed, but
this will persist through my very long life

I laugh, because this is a bummer, it really is
a myth, teenage

angst will persist, when I arrive home

Umma is splayed on her bed

pale without a blanket,
crab meat on a plate, a tender and

useless thing, a long life
stringing on her sheets   she tells me

she is 60 years old, so in the last three days
she's eaten nothing but burnt rice and barley tea

she wants to jump from somewhere very high,
but we only live on the second floor

her teeth are short and brittle and
she's had three root canals in the last year

I touch her belly, soft and cool
despite golden hour still

streaming on her skin
her stomach rumbles,

we couldn't plan this far ahead

south korea: an economic miracle

before, a wet gash
was the roof
and the dogs
were wild,
and we chased them
with brooms,
and my height
was average, and I sold
hard candies
by the road,
by the 매화's winter
blooms, and we
were children,
slim, we mimicked
a hungering
for something
intact–shoes, limbs,
a country–
white worms in my stomach.
in forty years,
a history
went
extinct

an afternoon in eze

a man humors me while I speak in French. I wonder of
inconvenience,
and space, and my body
situated at the crux
of this cobble staircase.
I've been reflecting on consumption. yesterday's pasta

was bouncy, and served by the chef who,
at some point, had chosen
the walls, the paint,   and I remember
my parents. the deli they owned, the radio's buzz,
the storefront was glass,
and blistered by lotto posters.

I am proud of where I am from.
            the aliveness of a packed space,
me shoveling through.
if this were home, I'd spot vivid
wrappers in each stone's crevice. beauty
is so easily marred.   I watch

the sea bend to the horizon. hazing white,
before gulping back into the sky.
                all of this exists
alongside credit card debt, student loans, the worsening climate.
foreign bugs who take interest in my flesh,
and I, at theirs.
running water. looping blood.
small havens, smelling of mineral.

migration

first warmth of the season the moon fully
unwaned   salamanders lift from hibernation and
there is a cotton black shirt in the trash
I got it with a friend I see once a year   if at all
it is warm and they move across the road in a sticking green clump
the mission is   to plant their eggs in hot vernal pools
across the road just a short distance a poster warns that inaction
is worse than a pack of cigarettes so
I walk forty minutes to Lucy's   something to learn is
not every salamander completes its crossing   some are faced
with tires   there are people I used to nap beside
legs draped atop mine
they rake me with such aching   or none at all

the lesson is   it's easy to wake up and   tiring
to fall asleep   my body whipping
hot in empty sheets   the duvet
too small for its cover   my pillow flattened by my weight
no matter the brand or my frequency of fluffing   friends
fall in love   and so do I
with a eucalyptus tree   its peeling bark   pale folds of skin

my mother tells me turtles are good luck

I knew a turtle who fell from a balcony whose shell cracked but did not shatter who lived for another five ten years and my mother asks my mother asks / *look at those claws thin and scraping? look at that mouth pruning like mine? look at that jaw that snaps like metal on a mouse's tail?* / look for a man who wants that, and keep looking keep looking keep looking keep looking keep looking keep looking keep looking keep

doing the dishes

I look like my mother, sobbing
in her yellow gloves.
outside, the metal gate
maintains a staggered wheeze.
pinching against the wind,
against its own hinges.

I lift a glass by its rim
and dare it to slip.
adulthood is cleaning surfaces
and holding your tongue.
folding the laundry,
brushing my bangs,

father gifts mother her most
hated flower.
unrolling the bouquet,
undressing its paper,
and snipping its ends.
a gift is an obligation—

a container of yellowed water
to replace, again,
the dropping of a petal,
orange and dry. I am
almost twenty-four,

the age of mother's first
miscarriage. I have her cheekbones
and full, sneering lips. a vase
of yellow lilies, outside the gate
is pleading
to burst.

beautiful country

in 미국,
imagine a mouth
stuffed white puckered pink
tender and sopping like
skin wrinkled around a bullet.

she migrated because
imagine her friend who was white whose
mother was alone because
imagine what she had to do
to that soldier
to have that much rice?

imagine she migrated because of how our tanks shone
how they glided along unpaved roads because
how effective they swept
bullets through her father's calf
as if suckled it sterile.

imagine how beautiful
the deepening of a finger.
the bullet that wades in foreign flesh. like
feet at the shore. like tide mounting
hardened wet like. mud crunching like
tasting pulled teeth.   and coughing out more

outside, it is 2 pm

the burst of light before the set. my big brother
snores from the basement. I hear him rise to
piss in a plastic bottle. I stitch
into the couch's gray upholstery. pondering, again,
how the winter sun masquerades as hot.
how we bear it.

SCENE

have you ever ingested a mosquito? hold your mouth open and inhale, swiftly. feel the substance squirm against the tug of your esophagus. its walls like a corn husk, crumbling off the grill. its lip, its needle, prodding for a grip, a puncture. and then, and then, swallow.

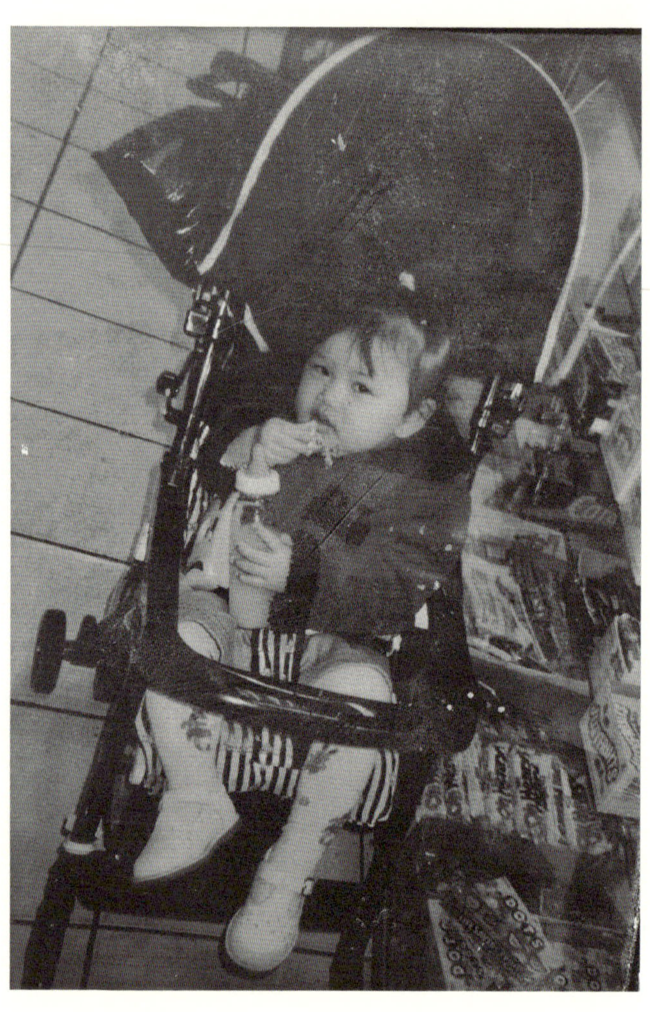

the neighborhood is changing

the night shift is in perfect English

a stroller by an ATM

Umma and Papa their stool by the radio

the cat on the sidewalk chewing on cold cuts

Equinox Starbucks

yesterday's paper

Papa comforts me a puddle murky

by the curb

the neighborhood is changing

Umma's stack of People magazine

american spirit   teddy grahams   trojans

mucinex   dollar lotto   sporks

an ATM

murky

by the curb

the neighborhood is changing

the night shift is   perfect.   streetlamps
    filter lotto posters. the refrigerator
is broken again. drunk
behind the deli. machine
slices body.
packaged turkey.   plain clothed cops.
aisles of metal.
                              thin scraps of skin.

the neighborhood is changing

cigarettes from Pakistan   illegal

but cheap.

many are visiting.
men ask for money.
women ask for more.
when Umma met Papa,
he offered her a soda   July
–four pm.
she returned hours later. when the air

was still hot. fireflies
pilled the concrete

the neighborhood is changing

what I'm showing you is perfect. to fall in love,
the aisles of metal and electricity bills.
men afraid of a child
because she is the boss's daughter, and the owner
is a bitch.   my parents met because they are immigrants,
and that is the closest they had to themselves.
            the life the self   must be created
of something greater
than violence

the neighborhood is changing

months or maybe a year, Umma slept
on a dog bed
we bought at Petco because
it was plushy,
and it sat
at the foot of my room
because an air mattress was too much work.

she slept there
for obvious reasons:
distance,
a locked door.
after
the night shift, Papa
tugged at the knob,
shook it and
screeched.
and she,   bleary,
worried I'd wake,

would enter the living room.

the neighborhood is changing

sometimes father would sleep for twenty hours.
these days Umma work double,
triple shifts. this is when she was cruel. I had
insomnia until twenty-two. until
I moved in with a woman
I hated. but
I could sleep, wrapped
in a body that despised mine
in turn. some
nights, when mother was not home. father
2am.
his silhouette over my bed
the light of the city behind him–
then
I would join him in the living room:
alone, alone, his voice clashes against nothing,
he'd say, pushing his hand
into the fishtank.
and caressing the body
inside. I
ignored this. his
pride. when he, during the day,
would ask to walk. I'd
hide
in the closet and he I
ignored when
he wanted to
burn it all down. close the stores and *give*
up

SCENE

we are older now, but not by much. this is important.

audible is the wisp of tires against concrete. the wind
between grasses, sounding like rain. the wide midwest
sky, which no longer scares me in its vast
unfamiliarity. my old gods are far from me now.
due to mileage, to time,

and yet the sight of them is constant.

there is a part of me that wants this.   cyan skies.
the first glimpse
of a stranger. before they clarify back
into a stranger. the clouds chugging across the sky
at an impossible distance. and me
searching upwards   for a face

when my father returned from work

it was my responsibility to peel back his crew-cut argyle socks.

previously, it was my mother who, upon hearing the click of the lock,
would cease the water's boiling
and he, as had rehearsed for 10,585 days,
would stomp onto our coffee table

(which doubled as a dining table
which doubled as a desk which, now,
doubled as a footrest)

and she, on her knees, would wrestle the faux leather from his feet,
suctioned due to moisture, and fold them methodically into a ribbon.

its odor wafted. a stale kind of cologne
that brought bile to my throat and   saliva
to the corners of my mouth. and I, head level to the bony
brownness of his big toe, dampness between my fingers,
inhaled. deeply.

after september

each bodega
each owned by a man
each named Mohammed.
dark blue clothing. FBI badges. glint of steel
they knock and my father never opens the door.
the door opens. and
          a shrew thrown overboard   its fur
sopping
he squeaks. the plastic couch.
sunken   I am not allowed in the living room
                              the coffee table scuffs
                    its varnish peels
shit floats up the fish tank.

after september
          cold silver stretches
across a slate gray table
a room tucked in an airport terminal
you've never heard of.   I arrive
my brother's luggage already inside out. still,
they rummage. squirrels after winter.
          i scrape. the skin. my thumb.
you look just like your mother
a red-bowed ribbon, zip-up sweater, Hello Kitty toothbrush
my mother's 노리개,
elastic tethered to two puffs

                                        so the men
                                        let me go.

how I learned to kill mosquitoes

I have gotten very good at killing
with a hard-bottom slipper or
Raid designed to spatter, pool, drown
roaches and ants.
I never kill
between my skin or with a napkin
never crunched lungs
clapped splat in thin white tissue
too close to its needle mouth
so I never will

wear skirts
except from age five to
seventeen, a little plaid hunter green
too long to be sexy, too short to be modest
so as soon as I got down the hallway
out of Umma's sight,
I rolled the waist exactly three times so
the hem would hit
above my fingertips. under that I wore
scratchy things, tights that always smelled
like pussy. my hole was out and this
was not sexy. maroon heeled oxfords and bright green tights I was
fourteen on a subway platform
at what could have been 4pm at 77th street
waiting, everyday, for the 6 train
when a suit dropped his briefcase,
I didn't help. I watched his papers puddle and
his nails scrape the muck
off the platform and he
on his knees and bits of blackened gum
from the charcoaled floor and I

watched him fail, over and
over again to lift the edge of the document.
I stood there, knees hip-width apart and thought,
I should help him.
he is Asian
and I am Asian
and I should but
anyway, it turns out this was all on purpose
that he tipped his bag and struggled too long
on purpose
while his phone faced upwards to film my

online I type "school-girl up-
skirt subway" and I watch
so many do not notice the
camera none of them
are wearing hot pink undies
bought on sale for $5 which is, in retrospect,
too expensive, but also
if I found the video
what could I even do but

kill it.
because it was buzzing and it was summer
and it landed on my wall.
sprayed it, hoping its body would limp and slip off.
it stayed stuck up there and it did not disintegrate
until December until I purchased
a very long stick from the Dollar Tree
attached to it a napkin and smacked. its body
fell so easily it
didn't leave a mark

much older, and very far away

Umma stood on the roof of the barn. it was raining,
she slipped
off its slanted edge.

but she was on her mountain. there,
she landed on all fours. there,
she splashed into mud,

and cackled. it was her mountain, her farm. once,
the whole family gathered,
because a pig had gone missing.

they gathered, then
dispersed over the mountainside. Umma
searched alone, lifting rocks, circling trees,

she knew trails with no markers.
she found it first,
a brown thing vibrating in a mesh of moss. the pig's

pink sockets gaped
into hers. they shared
a breath before it scurried. that night,

the whole family ate samgyupsal,
pork belly dipped in sea salt and vinegar,
then wrapped in fresh sesame leaf.

now, Umma grows sesame leaves in the window
of a crowded Bronx apartment.
she is watering them now. she is
transferring sink water from a green plastic cup

to a rectangular pot. she
groans, clutching the small of her back.
I rush to steady her.

she waves her hand to shoo me away.
she says, stop looking at me

like a mother.

american dream

so the deed is done
and I'm back alone.
this is called
a miracle:
my thinning hair
and fleshless hands
boiling barley
on a filthing
gas stove.
this strange
strange country,
less strange, now,
than my own—
Korea: a miracle,
unneeding of
remission.
unneeding of my
skin:
my sogging
wooden roof, my
molded towel,
overused.
I never thought
this would happen.
that I would die
as I was born.

SCENE

she is alive, and today,
her legs burst at the grill.
on the phone, *apeu apeu*
      but how is this possible?
just the other night
she called me with a grin:
like a friend,
she went *heyyyy baby*
and asked me
to renew her food stamps.

a thing that refuses to die

what is your father like?

everyone is older now.
there is a lot I remember—

the concave mound of his mouth.
grey speckled irises. smile lines, deep as
my own.

there is more I do not—

he was bad to my mother. he liked long walks. he drove fast. rum—the brown kind. he met my mother. first snow. he boarded my bedroom. he smacked a branch. I did not sleep. he cracked a tv. she shivered, damp. he was a shadow—a loud one. I liked him very much.

the good parts—

there's a lot I could remember.

everyone is older now.

when I left, I was fourteen, and there's a lot I

his face,
static.
still, I have aged.   when we left, my mother,

the good parts—

a mouse, crunched   *is supposed to die.*

a dustpan, ears still pink and still
twitching.

a boot, crunch.

the red parts—

scrape
up the sink.

squeeze
out the shower.

a   sound   sounds   soft   in   the   distance

jaan
meri jaan
his coos in my chest
without intention. a language I
some things
I still remember.
some things I wish
I couldn't.
some things are dead.
and still living.
some things
refuse
to die.

cicadas in the apartment I

I cannot have sex right now! I am busy
thinking about bugs.
how cold they must have been to confine
themselves to my apartment. when the earth dropped
in just six hours, and the red ones cannot reproduce indoors,
but can enjoy, in clusters, the west facing sun
through the window
while they are still able to do so.

the day will rear back in, and when it does,
I will convince the bugs out. all of them,
and their webbed glass wings.
I fear I am unable to perform
violence nor gentleness, I think,
eying the bug on the lace shower curtain. I know
someone who was once alive. organs
clung to the threading. open
insides. hostile
indoors. my pelvis
and images of men
who have been
alive
and will be   . palms
pressed to the skull
of an insect.
cold tile—
    spring

the moon in two phases

I tell her I was on the moon once before, and back then,
I thought I was in love. back then
I was on the shore
overstretched over a
foreign country. forming shapes with my tongue I
cannot remember. back then I wore sneakers
white air force ones.
and there was a sinkhole.
and there were oysters.
and I fell on my ass
while reaching for a shell, my heel caught
and thudded the sand. my wrists,
strangers
or acquaintances,
I was limp and hoisted and somehow,

tonight is January.
her blue carhartt jacket
her too many sweaters
her tide, shivering
her pebbles her seagulls
her nested on soft green shards.
it is evening,
the sand is kinetic.
we stand, knees buckled
a breath apart.
we are not in love
but her ears are pink,
her scarf around my neck.
we move
on this moon.
hovering a mound
and sliding down.
the fill of boots
is solid dusk. speak of
cotton in the oil-spill sky,
the thin black line at the base of her jaw.
she rubs her chin, clipped short.
I think of home
and the places we cannot go.
my nose drips.
I am embarrassed.

cicadas in the apartment II

I am always ending the story short. like
an overturned nest   knocked by wind
eggs   scrambling the
mother will return to massacre.
but will be alive, baying
            over the concrete. but I am rambling. I am   what I am
trying to say is:
they are alive—the bugs all thousands of them,
slid from my apartment the next easy morning as if to
chide me for melodrama. I

(a large, fleshy thing)   am always reducing myself
to the plight of women: indoors   anxious
to tug the knob so not to disturb
the cracks in the wood. all the life   in there:
carpenter ants, just burgeoning wasps, and those
            ghosts who have slammed that frame without care
yowling after the wife
en route to toss the trash.

            these are all the things I fear. life,
the potential, the memory.

I was trying to avoid cruelty, I cry,
kneeling at the window's glass. and I hear the bugs reply
in their high, monotoned chorus: *to*
acquiesce is not a form of power,
but another shred of cuticle
peeled back until dry,
stinging only at the moment of detachment. plucked skin
            —yes, that is skin, and that is my body it was attached to,
and there is a hard,

red wound under that slow,
frequent pilling.   the bugs

were born clawing
in herds out the earth. knowing
that a house sparrow,
            (a creature so pleasant I have paid it no mind)
will take its fill. unhinge its wings,
and soar with a body in the mouth. I saw this happen, so I know
it is real.   stained glass wings: an oasis
in concrete sprawl. the grass
chimes on,   metallic

strong feelings

a child bangs his forehead against the hardwood floor.
several purple bruises.
he holds his breath
until unconscious. the intention is
to alarm the parent.
the refusal or inability
to articulate
desire. pick me
up. I want
a rising
chest. a hand
to my cheek.
my chin. let
me out
of this crib.
give me
that banana,
the singing caterpillar,
the toy with yellow rings

pulling hair out the tub

that one touched me like a bathtub drain
scraping the contours   without aggression
and with some force. I have never been as known
as the headied breath of the orgasm, plucking a hair
before pulling his mouth toward mine. this is the cost
of mimicking connection. I do not
fault him for not loving me   the way
I do not love myself   bulbous
in that mesh wire trapping. those strands
were my body, and I have treated it terribly.
the trash is flush
with cotton, still warm from my body,
and I regard it with disgust.   I have learned
that some attention is worse than neglect:
               I have not starved, but have withheld so to thin,
worn shoes that crush the edge of my feet, endured
burn for the prospect of aloe. a nest of flies
has collected under the tub
and they are, miraculously,
alive. I tried
to prevent this, toweling what I could
of the standing pool. but some
survived, those flecks of being,
born buzzing and
               slamming into the cupboard

buying new school clothes

I have just finished tearing off my lips
and am rushing to greet Mother at the door.
she asks if I want to go to TJ Maxx.
I squawk something gnarled, unable to enunciate
due to the jagged gap in my face. she laughs,
don't be like that, you need new clothes for school.

I take her hand and walk to the next room.

alone sits Father in the living room,
shirtless on a long black chaise.
his pepper chest curls above his beer belly. his face is pregnant,
he looks straight ahead.
he does not acknowledge my body in the entrance.
does not notice my lack of mouth.
you know, beti, I would never hurt anyone.
not even your mother.

I exit the room.

now Mother is standing in the apartment hallway,
holding up two shopping bags.
don't tell your father about these bags!
he is unruly when we spend the money.
I am glad my lips are gone, and far from scabbing over.
I do not like
to make mistakes. I recall a time
before I had resigned to calamity. I'd beg for reason,
and gnaw my lip,
as I did with my cuticles
before I had picked them to nubs.

and Mother is still before me, a bag in each hand.
her holey orange shirt hangs off her skin.
it has worn her since before she conceived,
and it has stretched,
or she has shrunk—
        she looks so tiny in this house.

and I grunt a nod, and tuck the bags under my shirt.

I must cross the living room to get to my bedroom. Father is
in the living room, and he has tripled in size.
his receding hair tickles the ceiling, he has tripled
in size, but his eyes
are still small.

my teeth fit perfect like exposed brick and
I clench until one dislodges.
I toss
the front one in his direction.
his elephant ears perk
and his body
clamors toward the clack.
I pry out another, and another,
and hurl them both,
and repeat the process.

he is further now, lifting the couch, running
his bloated hand over the hardwood floor.
I am almost to the bedroom door.
but the plastic crinkles
under my shirt.
he hears me.
now he runs in my direction,
shaking the furniture, the ceramic pots, the silverware rumbles
off its surfaces.

I release a sound.

he does not hear it. Mother appears
and pleads, *it was me, I bought it.*
so I sound harder, I push myself between them, they thrash
against each other,

but their hands push through me.
I had chewed off my arms, my lips, my chest, my
          am just eyes and ears.

after ten years

I observe my brother gentle
    as his children stumble
the foundations of living: eating, sleeping,
    shitting, cartoons, and all at once,
the sun grasps onto a new, continuous blue. it's irreversible
    I comprehend
mortality. many evenings
    and a whole, brief life
I spent with him on a living room couch,
    laughing wordlessly to a show I did not select.
and here we are again. grown
    sitting opposite in a rental home. swarming
days and many children, that world
    and its rounded palms,
existed only once, and only for us.
    out the window, a woodpecker beats,
but right here, the children want smoothie pouches.
    tomorrow, they will board a plane
and I will watch as my brother, his children, that
    whole world
obscure the horizon

what we have done

the world is a collection of scenes. violent
teals. a prophet formed
of sea foam. this morning I watched a gull
butcher a pigeon on the roof of a van,
churning under eighty degree heat. and I thought,
          I have seen this before—
tendons that attach wing to wing, laid bare and red
by a sharp stretching mouth.
elastic of tissue, somehow void of blood. where purple folds ripe
over blue. men, the square reflection
of a goat's eye.   I am happy here
with my gorged stomach and daily tasks.
the earth is rolling itself up a hill
          and in it, a spider drips
at its own creation.
long hair clutches a lily blanket,
and in it,
a body replaces a life.
          beside all goodness is more of the same—dark hues
of repetition. engines bring clouds to the concrete.
yet I am standing here
wanting more

lake michigan, 2025

the boys and girls are making violence
under the brush,
where the current works itself at the shore.

    I fear I see meaning in every act,
the squirrel watching devilishly on its hind legs. I split

my life in three ways: talking to you
chewing my fingernails
and thinking about being young.

I also concern myself
with adult woman topics:

    the joy of the steamer
a new lint brush, and men, wondering, why! did the man

when? will the man?
then, it doesn't matter. what the man.

I waste time
at the park,   searching for delight. many friends

are marrying now, and although I do not envy,
I fear I am falling behind. the other day

I sought to identify a bird
which chimed from low, round tree

and was interrupted by a woman
gagging heinously at two pm

as a kind man rubbed her back.
when I was 19, and when I was younger,

and when I was also older,
I learned many wrong lessons.

I'm sorry if you already know this,

but Lake Michigan is so vast
it has its own current? and when it is cold,
and the lake freezes over, so do the waves?

and under that, still movement,
biting against the surface.

I want to see that very badly.
the steam made by motion. pain by numbness.
stung fingers bare in the impossible cold. sometimes

the wind is so strong
it is a hand to the sternum. pressed wholly,
entering the mouth, and choking.

each time, this makes me feel less alive.

the body not gasping,   but enduring until release.

I saw a mother and daughter holding hands

she no longer asks me how school is going,
or what outfits are in.
what I ate today, and how I afforded it.
what my friends are up to, or if a boy
has *said anything nice to you.*
    old gossip, and no more
talk of weddings. we are
a blister, drained.
thin skin,
cavernously raised,
and hinged to something
about to heal over.

해녀 ("diving women")

how tiring it is to be
without use   there are mothers
of Jeju who have gone   obsolete   age, industry
but they are still honored   with statues, newspaper articles
they are women over eighty with the widest lungs
skin with the heft to endure   the most frigid waters
in just   a cotton jumper   hands
to sealife's liquid bodies   how deeply we yearn
for touch   when I stand at the shore   clams huddle
towards the warmth of a recent footstep
then are taken back   where salt crashes over
the shell   is not a casket   the shell
is repurposed   as dust   repurposes my bedroom
when I was young   I thought the way
to die was one's own hand   the daughters
of diving women   tire   of training not to drown
I wish I wanted   more
from you

the women

that day you died.
that day lasted twelve years.
there is nothing
more than this. cut
flowers. still yellow
waters. ripe
scent of rot. what is left
to mourn the living? the daughter
cheek slumped to
the lover's breast. the seabird
twisted at
the neck. the ocean
reaching toward
itself. the nautilus
living.

life as pendulum

november is time for departure. you,
you, and you again—a year ago,
I wrapped my lips   around an ashtray
to taste the last scores of your mouth. adoration
is not unlike degradation.

I will not explain this further.

reader, lover, new boss or acquaintance,
just—be certain of this:
there is no better life than the present.
              my sheets are orange, and the wind
so desperate to meet my window,
to let seep the hum of newly crackled leaves.
the plane overhead
does not make me afraid—at times,
I've thought viscously
of the end: when mother, from a leaking skull
                   when brother, from opiates
                   when father, from want—
     snow, snow, and snow again
in time, leaves will be made   anonymous.
a car will erupt
      at a headlight,
      or a woman, clutching
the edge of her puffer coat,
frenzied in the dandruff of beams
then will hurry on   again

learning nothing.

Acknowledgements

Thank you to the journals that feature earlier versions of these works:

Epiphany Magazine: "these are just a few" "the neighborhood is changing" and "much older, and very far away"

Tupelo Quarterly: "everything returns to itself" "I am every mirror" "strong feelings" "the moon in two phases" and "life as pendulum"

Gab Magazine: "pulling hair out the tub"

Jet Fuel Review: "the women" and "how I learned to kill mosquitoes"

"how I learned to kill mosquitoes" was awarded an honorary mention by American Academy of Poets

Cagibi Lit: "South Korea: An Economic Miracle"

Passengers Journal: "and I lived there" and "해녀"

'해녀' was nominated for Best of the Net 2025
'해녀' was a finalist for the West Trade Review poetry contest

The Worcester Review: "doing the dishes"

Pigeon Pages: "a palm reader tells me I will live a long and healthy life"

Asian American Writers' Workshop The Margins: "after september"

The Berkeley Poetry Review: "a thing that refuses to die"

"when my father returned from work" and "sharp breath" first appeared in *MON-monuments, monarchs, and monsters* (Sputnik & Fizzle, 2020)

Thank you to my mother, who has supported my writing with enthusiasm and warmth.

Danielle Vogel for her long-term mentorship.

Stephen Gould Rose, Ann Scott Knight, and Allison Albino—grade school teachers who saw promise in my writing.

My MFA professors, including my thesis advisor, Timothy Donnelly, for knowing this book before it was a book.

My publisher, Whitney Koo, for her expansive collaboration.

The poets I met in grad school who know my work better than anyone—Kai-Lilly Karpman, Heather Gluck.

And everyone who has loved me when times were tough or fantastic. Of which there are too many to name.

Mina Khan is a Korean-Pakistani American poet from NYC, based currently out of Chicago. Her writing spans across nations, generations, to discuss cyclicality, violence, tenderness, and the everyday. Her work has appeared in AAWW's *The Margins, Tupelo Quarterly, Epiphany Magazine,* and more. Khan holds a BA from Wesleyan University, MFA from Columbia University, and is a Tin House alum. This is her debut collection.